Paul Robeson

Nick Healy

Chicago, Illinois

For information, address the publisher
Raintree, 100 N. LaSalle, Suite 1200, Chicago, IL 60602

Printed and bound in the United States at Lake Book Manufacturing, Inc.
07 06 05 04 03
10 9 8 7 6 5 4 3 2 1

Library of Congress Cataloging-in-Publication Data

Healy, Nick.
  Paul Robeson / Nick Healy.
    v. cm. -- (African American biographies)
  Includes bibliographical references (p.) and index.
  Contents: Family and youth -- A man on his own -- An international star
-- A man of principles -- Troubled times -- Later years -- Robeson's
place in history -- Glossary.
  ISBN 0-7398-6874-8 (HC), 1-4109-0040-1 (Pbk.)
  1. Robeson, Paul, 1898-1976--Juvenile literature. 2. African
Americans--Biography--Juvenile literature. 3. Actors--United
States--Biography--Juvenile literature. 4. Singers--United
States--Biography--Juvenile literature. 5. Political activists--United
States--Biography--Juvenile literature. [1. Robeson, Paul, 1898-1976. 2.
Actors and actresses. 3. Singers. 4. Political activists. 5. African
Americans--Biography.] I. Title. II. Series: African American
biographies (Chicago, Ill.)

E185.97.R63H43 2003
782'.0092--dc21
                                        2002153813

Acknowledgments
The publishers would like to thank the following for permission to reproduce photographs:
pp. 4, 22 Hulton/Archive by Getty Images; pp. 6, 8, 14, 26, 30, 36, 38, 43, 44, 46, 48, 51, 53, 55, 59 Bettmann/CORBIS; pp. 10, 33 CORBIS; p. 17 Joel Katz/CORBIS; pp. 21, 24, 29, 35 Underwood & Underwood/CORBIS; pp. 41, 56 Hulton-Deutsch Collection/CORBIS.

Cover photograph: Hulton-Deutsch Collection/CORBIS

Content Consultant
Andrew J. Furer, Ph.D.
Assistant Professor of Humanities and Rhetoric
College of General Studies
Boston University

Some words are shown in bold, **like this.** You can find out what they mean by looking in the Glossary.

Contents

Paul Robeson stars in the Shakespearian play Othello *in London in 1959.*

Introduction

Paul Robeson was a man of many talents. He was an excellent student. He was a sports star. He could sing. He could act. It seemed like there was nothing he could not do. However, his many skills did not make him a great and famous person. His hard work did that.

He began life as the son of a preacher. His family endured difficult times during his childhood. His mother died tragically when he was only five. Despite hardships, though, Robeson succeeded at almost everything he tried. His high school years were filled with achievement in classes, clubs, and sports. In college he was one of the greatest football players of his time. But sports did not crowd out his other interests. He studied hard and graduated from law school.

Surprisingly, Robeson never became famous for being a lawyer. Instead, it was acting and singing that introduced him to the world. After college he quickly became a star on the stage. He acted in

In 1949, in Paris, France, Robeson told a group called the World Congress of the Partisans of Peace that African Americans would never fight against the Russians because the people of Russia treated black people as equals.

plays that became hits in New York and London. Some of them were made into movies, and he became a star on the big screen, too. Robeson also devoted himself to music. He gave concerts all over the world. He liked to sing the songs of common folks. Robeson especially loved to perform traditional music of African-American people. Crowds of all races went to hear him sing, and the music helped bring people together.

He cared about poor and unfortunate people everywhere. He led protests to help those people. He fought against laws that were unfair to African Americans and other people of color, and tried to stop violence against them. He tried to help people in need in Africa, India, and elsewhere. He became one of the most famous and respected African Americans alive.

Later in his life, Robeson faced hard times again. Some things he believed had become unpopular in the United States. Some people tried to make him change his views. But Robeson stayed true to himself. He made it through those hard times, too.

From the 1920s to the 1950s, Robeson was one of the most famous people in the country. Today he is not remembered as well as other African-American leaders of his time. But he cannot be overlooked. His life was rich with many achievements. His work helped improve the lives of many others. He stood by his beliefs and never gave up on his dreams.

Throughout his life, actor and singer Paul Robeson fought against racial prejudice and discrimination against African Americans. He was born on April 9, 1898, in Princeton, New Jersey.

Chapter 1:
Family and Youth

Paul Robeson's life began in Princeton, New Jersey, in a small house alongside a church. His father was the preacher at the church. Paul's parents and five siblings were very close and they all believed in equal rights for African Americans. They did not want racial **prejudice** to hold them down.

Family History

Robeson's father was born in 1845. His full name was William Drew Robeson. He was a slave on a **plantation** in North Carolina. His childhood home was a tiny cabin. It had only one room and no windows. Life was very difficult.

When he was a teenager, William decided to run away. That was a risky thing for a slave to do. If runaway slaves were caught, they faced terrible punishment. Many slave owners used a whip to punish runaways.

This Civil War victory parade took place along Pennsylvania Avenue in Washington, D.C., on May 23, 1865. People were celebrating the fact that the United States would remain a unified country.

But William was desperate to be free. He used all his courage to run away, and he was not captured. The year was 1860, and the Civil War (1860–1864) between the North and the South was about to begin.

The next year William joined the army of the North. He was among many African Americans who fought on the side of the North against the army of the South. All slaves were freed after the South was finally defeated in 1864.

William lived in Pennsylvania after the war. That is where he studied to become a preacher. That is also where he met Maria Louisa Bustill, a schoolteacher. She was born in 1853 and grew up in Philadelphia. Her family background included African Americans, Cherokee Indians, and whites. William and Maria were married in 1878. They moved to Princeton the next year.

Childhood Years

Robeson was born in Princeton on April 9, 1898. There is a very famous university there called Princeton University. When Robeson was born, the university was for whites only. Not until July 24, 1945, was a black student admitted there.

Robeson's parents were well known in town. His father was the pastor at Witherspoon Street Presbyterian Church. Every Sunday many members of the town's African-American community went to hear him preach.

Paul was the youngest child of William and Maria. He had three brothers and one sister.

Tragedy Strikes

When Paul Robeson was a small child, his family faced hard times. The trouble began when Robeson was only one year old. There was a dispute among members of William Robeson's church. He lost his job as pastor. Robeson and his family had to move out of the house the church had provided for them. Robeson's father had no work, and the family had no home.

The events saddened Robeson's father, but he went right to work. He used a horse-drawn wagon to haul away ash from coal furnaces. People in Princeton paid to have the dirty job done for them. The Robesons found a new place to live.

Several years later Robeson's mother was killed in an accident at the family's home. She had been cleaning near a stove when a hot coal fell on her dress. Maria's eyesight was very poor. She did not notice the coal until it was too late. One of her older children was home at the time, but he could not save her from burning. At the time Robeson was just five years old.

School Days

Robeson's father had to raise his children alone after the tragic accident. He believed that education was the most important thing in life. He kept them busy with books, lessons, and games.

The family moved twice during Robeson's years in grade school. They were living in Somerville, New Jersey, when Robeson began high school at age fourteen. Robeson was one of three African Americans at Somerville High School in 1912. The rest of the 250 students were white.

Robeson thrived at the school. He was a sports star. Football was his best game, but he also won letters in baseball, basketball, and track. He also joined the school drama club. He was curious about acting and got an important part in the school play. Robeson was very nervous during the show, and he did not know if he ever wanted to be on stage again.

Robeson's father wanted his son to go to college, but he was concerned about the cost. Then the Robesons heard about a **scholarship** offered by Rutgers College (later named Rutgers University). Rutgers was a small private school located close to the Robesons' home.

Each year, Rutgers offered a free college education to one student from New Jersey. The student who scored the highest on two tests was awarded the scholarship. But when Robeson first heard about the scholarship, he had already missed the first test covering the first three years of high school. Nobody at Somerville High thought to tell Robeson about it. People liked him, but it did not occur to them that a black person could get a scholarship.

In the spring of 1915, most seniors sat down to be tested on their final year of high school. Robeson had to be tested on all four years at once. With help from his father, Robeson studied daily to prepare for the test. He managed to get the highest score in the state. He went to Rutgers in the fall.

This Rutgers quarterback is about to throw the ball in a game versus Princeton in 1914. Robeson would become a star player on the Rutgers team a year later.

Chapter 2:
A Man on His Own

College life changed everything for Paul Robeson. He was on his own for the first time. He moved away from his home and his father. He and his father were very close, and his father had always helped to guide him through life.

Robeson also had to leave behind Somerville High School. He was one of just a few African Americans at the school. Even so, those students were treated with courtesy by their white classmates.

But Robeson discovered that attitudes at Rutgers University were very different. Only two other African Americans had been students at Rutgers in the 150 years before Robeson arrived. He was one of only two African Americans on campus when he began classes in the fall of 1915. All of the other 500 students were white. Robeson was not allowed to live on campus with other students. The dormitory where students lived was for whites only. In those days many whites believed in **segregation.** Segregation means forcing people of different races to live apart from each other. Because of segregation many African Americans had to go to separate schools. They also had to eat at separate restaurants and stay in separate hotels. Many businesses had signs that said "Whites Only." Robeson stayed with an African-American family who lived near Rutgers.

Athletic Challenges and Victories

Robeson ran into trouble when a coach allowed him to play for the Rutgers football team. Many white players did not want him around. Players went after Robeson during a scrimmage on the first day of practice. One player punched Robeson and broke his nose. As Robeson lay on the ground, other players kicked and kneed him. The punishment did not stop there. White players beat up on him again when he returned to practice a few days later.

Robeson grew very angry. He picked up one of the white players and lifted him over his head. Robeson was prepared to slam the player to the ground, but the coach stopped him. The coach was impressed by Robeson's strength and determination. Right then he told Robeson he would play varsity that year. It was a rare accomplishment for a freshman.

Duing segregation, "colored" was a term many people used when talking about African Americans, as seen in this 1964 photo of a food stand. Today, "colored" is considered derogatory, which means it is offensive to use it when referring to anyone.

It turned out to be a wise move by the coach. Robeson was a great college player. Eventually he was admired by his teammates. He was loved by fans, who liked to call him "Robey." He was named an All-American twice, meaning he was among the best college players in the nation.

People around the country noticed the great young athlete at Rutgers. Robeson also did well in other sports. He was a star catcher on the baseball team. He played center on the basketball squad. He excelled in track and field. In all, Robeson won 15 letters in four sports during his years at Rutgers.

Still, he could not escape **segregation.** In 1916, the football team from Washington and Lee College refused to play against an African American. The Rutgers coach told Robeson he could not play, and the game went on. But the coach felt bad about his decision and never kept Robeson out of a game again.

Another Death in the Family

Sad news came from home during Robeson's junior year of college. His father had grown very ill. William Robeson was 73 years old. He died on May 17, 1918. Before he died, William made Paul promise not to cancel his plans to compete in a speech contest a few days later, which Paul wanted to do out of respect for his father. The contest was for the best speaker in the student body. Robeson kept his promise and won the contest.

Famous Words of Paul Robeson

"The artist must elect to fight for Freedom or for Slavery. I have made my choice. I had no alternative."—1937

"My father was a slave, and my people died to build this country, and I am going to stay here and have a piece of it, just like you." —1956

"I am the same old Paul, dedicated as ever to the cause of humanity for freedom, peace, and brotherhood."—1973

Robeson graduated from Rutgers the next spring. He was chosen by classmates to be the class valedictorian. He gave a speech at the graduation ceremony. The topic of his speech was the need for laws that treat all people fairly, without regard to the color of their skin.

Moves to Harlem

Robeson wanted to become a lawyer. He believed that this would help him fight laws that were unfair to African Americans. After leaving Rutgers, Robeson moved to New York City. He entered law school at Columbia University in 1920.

He found a place to live in Harlem, which is a large section of New York City. Most of the people who lived in Harlem were

African Americans. At that time, Harlem might have been the most exciting place in the world for people of color.

Robeson saw a place where African Americans thrived. People worked hard and lived well. African-American artists were popular there. Singers and performers of all kinds drew big crowds. Robeson performed for black and white audiences at Harlem theaters and clubs.

In 1920 Robeson met a woman named Eslanda Goode. She was called Essie by her friends. She was also a student at Columbia. Robeson proposed to Essie a short time later, and they were married in 1921.

A New Career

Essie urged her husband to try acting again. She convinced him to try out for a part in a play called *Simon the Cyrenian* put on by the Harlem YMCA (Young Men's Christian Association). Robeson got the part. He did it to please his wife, but people noticed his talent.

Soon he had his first professional acting job. That meant he was paid to play his part. The play was called *Taboo*. It opened in New York in 1922, and then moved to England. Robeson spent one summer in England. The show moved from town to town. Newspaper writers gave the play good reviews. Many of them praised Robeson in particular.

A doorman stands in front of the Cotton Club, one of the most popular nightclubs in Harlem between 1920 and 1940.

Robeson never left his legal studies. In 1923, he graduated from law school. He was hired at a New York law firm, but the white staff members made him feel unwelcome. A white secretary refused to type a letter for him. She said she would never take orders from an African American. Robeson left the firm that day and never returned. He was no longer excited about being a lawyer. Robeson believed he belonged on stage.

Paul Robeson plays a character named Bustill in 1925 in Eugene O'Neill's play Emperor Jones.

Chapter 3: An International Star

Success filled the next several years of Paul Robeson's life. He rose to fame quickly. He acted in several plays. He performed for larger audiences in larger theaters. Robeson's popularity grew steadily. He also did well as a singer. His concert tours pleased crowds in the United States and Europe.

His life changed in many ways. He traveled to many countries. He saw how people lived around the world. He became a father. But he still had to deal with **segregation.** It did not matter how famous he became. It did not matter how much money he earned. Racial **prejudice** still made life difficult.

On Stage and Screen

In 1924 Robeson played parts in two plays. Both were written by a man named Eugene O'Neill. O'Neill wrote some of the greatest plays of his time. Robeson was paid $75 a week for his work. That was a good paycheck in those days. The plays were called *The Emperor Jones* and *All God's Chillun' Got Wings*.

Robeson, hands in the air, is surrounded by ghosts in the 1933 production of The Emperor Jones.

All God's Chillun' Got Wings caused quite a stir even before it was performed. Robeson played an African-American man with a white wife. That alone was enough to upset some white people. At the end of the play, the wife kissed the hand of her husband. That outraged some whites. Newspapers said the play could cause riots and trouble between whites and African Americans, but luckily nothing like that happened.

Robeson was very busy that year. He also performed in his first musical concert, and he acted in his first movie. The film was a silent movie called *Body and Soul*. It was directed by another African American. It was not a hit, but it was a good start.

Singing Traditional Songs

Robeson was standing on a corner in New York one day in 1925. He happened to see Lawrence Brown. The two had first met years earlier in London. Robeson and Brown sat down to talk after seeing each other on the street.

Brown was a pianist and a composer, that is, someone who writes music. Brown was especially fond of traditional African-American songs, or **spirituals**. One of the most famous spirituals is "Swing Low, Sweet Chariot." Robeson liked these songs, too. They decided to give a concert together.

The old songs had been passed down from generation to generation. Parents taught their children the words to the spirituals. Many African Americans enjoyed singing and hearing the songs. However, they were not the kind of songs performed in formal concerts. Brown and Robeson wanted to change that. They also wanted to introduce African-American songs to people of all colors.

Robeson belts out an African-American spiritual, as his friend Lawrence Brown accompanies him on the piano.

Their first performance was held in New York in 1925. There had never been a concert like it. Robeson sang sixteen old **spirituals.** The large crowd was thrilled. Brown and Robeson were soon asked to record the songs. They began planning a concert tour of the United States.

Living with Segregation

Before the tour began, Robeson returned to London to be in another play. It was *The Emperor Jones*, the Eugene O'Neill play he had been in a year earlier in New York. The London crowds were dazzled by Robeson.

Robeson and his wife were happy in London. They enjoyed living away from the **segregation** in the United States. They could go to any restaurant they liked. They could stay at the hotel of their choice. London businesses did not have whites-only rules.

Early in 1926 Robeson returned to the United States to begin the concert tour. Robeson and Brown set out to perform spirituals on the East Coast and in the Midwest. The concerts were hits in every city along the way. People of all colors flocked to theaters when Robeson and Brown performed. Robeson hoped the songs would build understanding between the races.

Just how does one say Paul Robeson's name?

In 1933 someone sent him a letter asking that question. Here is what he wrote in response:

"The name is Robeson: Robe as in the ordinary word, robe, meaning dress, and son pronounced like the word son, meaning a male child. The name is pronounced in two syllables only: Robe-son."

In many ways, the tour was difficult for Robeson. He was troubled by **segregation** in many cities. He was turned away from hotels and restaurants. Even restrooms were for whites only in some places. Robeson was a famous star, but even he could not get past the "whites only" signs.

A Baby in the Family

In 1927 Robeson and his wife got some happy news. Their first baby was on the way. Robeson continued to work while Essie stayed in New York. She prepared for the baby with the help of her mother, who had come to live at the Robesons' home.

Brown and Robeson continued to perform the **spirituals.** They toured more U.S. cities. Later that year, they began a tour of cities in Europe. The first show was in Paris, and it was sold out. A crowd of French people went to hear the old African-American songs.

Robeson was still in Paris when his son was born. The baby came on November 2, 1927. He was named Paul Junior. Robeson and Essie called him by the nickname Pauli. He would be their only child.

The next year Robeson brought his family to London. He was there to be in a play called *Show Boat*. The character he played sang "Ol' Man River," a song that was perfect for his powerful voice. It was the highlight of the show. Robeson made the song famous.

Robeson acts in the movie Show Boat, *a hit based on the play where he made the song "Ol' Man River," famous.*

The Robesons decided to live in London to get away from segregation. Essie said they were treated with respect in London. They could dine wherever they liked, she said. London was not entirely free of racism, but the Robeson family was happy there for awhile.

In 1931, people gather outside of a bank that has closed because of the Great Depression. Many people lost all of their money during the 1930s.

Chapter 4:
A Man of Principles

In the 1930s, the United States and other nations experienced a dark time. That period in history is called the **Great Depression.** Millions of people were trapped in poverty. Misery in the lives of so many caused a rise in racism and hatred, because some tried to blame their problems on groups of people unlike themselves.

The Great Depression cost millions of Americans their jobs in the 1930s. Many companies went out of business. Banks had to shut down. People were poor and hungry. Hard times also hit England, and many people lost their jobs. A powerful new leader with disturbing ideas was in charge of Germany. There was political trouble in many places, including Spain, Italy, and parts of Asia and Africa. It was becoming impossible to ignore the struggles so many people faced. War was around the corner.

For years Robeson had been an outspoken supporter of the African-American community and people of color everywhere. He supported the arts and culture of African Americans. His concerts introduced thousands to their songs and traditions.

But starting in the 1930s, Robeson started to think about the world differently. He studied the history and culture of Africa. He also studied about Jewish people. He read about the Russians and the Irish, too. He decided that all people were more alike than different. He began to be interested not just in African Americans, but in the lives of the poor and suffering all around the world.

Common People, Common Problems

Robeson grew very concerned when he saw what was going on in the world. Many leaders did not treat all people equally. Some leaders allowed whole groups of people to suffer. A few leaders even caused this suffering. In Germany, Adolf Hitler and his **Nazi Party** had taken control. The **Nazis** blamed Jewish people for the hard times in Germany. Hitler was starting a violent effort to rid the country of Jewish people.

Robeson was upset by what the Nazis were doing in Germany. He believed that African Americans and Jewish people had much in common. Both had long been the victims of **prejudice.** Robeson said that the Nazis' treatment of Jews was the worst thing the world had seen in centuries.

Nazi leader Adolf Hitler celebrates on March 13, 1938, a day after the German Army occupied Austria.

He still gave many concerts featuring the old African-American **spirituals.** In the 1930s, though, he began to sing Jewish folksongs in his concerts, as well. Folk music from other countries interested Robeson. He wanted to show that common people everywhere faced many of the same challenges.

Traveling and Learning

In 1934 Robeson took a trip to meet a film director in Moscow, which was the biggest city in the **Soviet Union.** The Soviet Union was a large and powerful country. Most of the land that was part of the old Soviet Union is now part of Russia.

Robeson traveled through Germany on his way to the Soviet Union. He saw how the **Nazis** hated all people who were not like them. They hated Jews because of their religion. They hated black people because of the color of their skin. Nazi soldiers threatened Robeson at a train station in the capital of Germany. They also followed him on the streets. He was relieved to get out of Germany safely.

Things were different in the Soviet Union. The situation there pleased Robeson. He believed that all people were treated fairly under Soviet **communism.** He said it was the first time he had seen true equality. As he toured the country, crowds cheered him.

Film Frustrations

Robeson acted in many movies during the 1930s, but he was not happy. He wanted the movies to show African Americans in a positive way. He also wanted to show African Americans as they really lived. He thought that too often films showed only negative **stereotypes.** A stereotype is a fixed idea about how people behave.

Paul Robeson starred in Sanders of the River *with Nina Mae McKinney, 1935.*

In 1935 Robeson starred in a movie he hoped would be different. The movie was called *Sanders of the River.* It took place in Africa. Robeson played an African king. He wanted the movie to show African customs and culture. However, he was not happy with the movie in the end. He said it made Africans seem like children who needed whites to care for them.

Thurgood Marshall, Robeson's neighbor and friend, talks to others at a meeting of the National Association for the Advancement of Colored People (NAACP) in Atlanta, Gerogia. He was a judge for the NAACP before he was chosen to serve as a justice on the U.S. Supreme Court.

Finally Robeson announced that he was done with movies. He would no longer be in films that showed only stereotypes. Robeson was not away from movies for long, but he made his point. In the late 1930s, he was in several films that he believed treated African Americans fairly. One such film was called *Proud Valley,* in which Robeson played a black coal miner who saves the lives of his white fellow miners.

The Verge of War

Robeson lived outside of the United States for several years. However, he never stopped calling himself an American citizen. In 1939 German armies invaded their peaceful neighbor Poland. World War II (1939–1945) had begun. Robeson was still living in London, but he rushed his family back to safety in New York.

He continued to battle racism and violence in many ways. He recorded a song called "The Ballad for Americans," which would become his most popular work. The patriotic song topped the charts in 1940. Robeson liked the song because it called for friendship between blacks and whites.

Robeson, his wife, and their son moved back into Harlem. They shared a neighborhood with many famous African Americans, including Thurgood Marshall, Roy Wilkins, and Langston Hughes. Marshall was a lawyer who later became a U.S. Supreme Court justice. Wilkins helped lead the movement to obtain equal rights for African-Americans. Hughes was a famous poet and writer.

Robeson gave concerts around the country in 1940. He refused to play for **segregated** audiences, so African Americans and whites had equal access to his shows. In Chicago a massive crowd of 160,000 gathered to hear him. He was a great artist who used his powerful voice to fight for his beliefs.

When the Japanese attacked Pearl Harbor on December 7, 1941, Robeson knew he had to do something to help his country. Here, the battleship USS Arizona sinks after being bombed during the surprise attack.

Chapter 5:
Troubled Times

Until 1941 Robeson had hoped the United States could stay out of the war. Two things happened that year to change his mind. First the German army attacked the **Soviet Union.** Then Japan attacked U.S. forces at Pearl Harbor in Hawaii.

Robeson wanted to help the United States. It was his homeland, and he cared deeply about the American people. He also cared about the Soviet Union. Robeson had admired the Soviets ever since his trip there in 1934. He liked the way they treated all people equally regardless of color.

The war gave Robeson a chance to support people he cared about. He gave many concerts to raise money for people in need. He helped people in the United States and in faraway countries. Millions of people respected and admired him.

War Years

America was involved in World War II from 1941 to 1945. Those years were very busy for Robeson. He continued to work as an actor on the stage and in movies. He also gave many benefit concerts.

Robeson traveled around the country to perform in 1941 and 1942. He also gave speeches urging cooperation among people of all colors. He had to be away from his wife and son for long periods of time. Essie and Paul Jr. went to live in Enfield, Connecticut, where Robeson had purchased a large home.

His acting career hit another high point in 1943. Robeson had a part in a play by William Shakespeare, *Othello*. The play has been famous for hundreds of years. It is a story about an African general who is betrayed by white friends. Robeson played the role of the general. The play was a hit on Broadway in New York. Newspapers raved about Robeson's acting.

When not on stage, Robeson kept talking about issues he cared about. A speech he gave in New York in 1943 got a lot of attention. Robeson was speaking at a forum about current problems. A New York newspaper sponsored the event.

In his speech Robeson talked about his visits to the **Soviet Union.** He praised the Soviets for treating all people with respect. At that time, the Soviet Union was a friend of the United States. The countries were working together to defeat Germany, Japan, and other enemies.

Othello

It is almost as if William Shakespeare had Paul Robeson in mind when he wrote *Othello.*

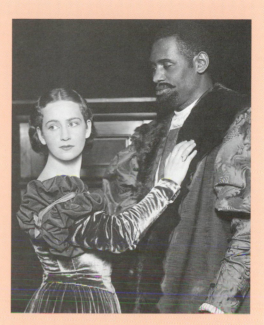

That's impossible, of course. Shakespeare died hundreds of years before Robeson was even born. But Robeson was great in Shakespeare's play. He was so great that it seemed as though the part had been created especially for him.

Photographed in London in 1929, here is Robeson as Othello with his co-star, the English actress Peggy Ashcroft.

Othello is Shakespeare's story of an African general. Shakespeare was an English playwright. In the years around 1600, he wrote many famous plays. *Romeo and Juliet* and *Hamlet* may be his best-known plays. However, *Othello* also remains popular.

Robeson was the first black actor to play Othello with a white supporting cast in an American production of the play. Before Robeson came along, white actors often played the part of the African general. The actors would put on black makeup. It was insulting to many African Americans. But Robeson changed that.

Robeson remained very popular as the end of the war neared. In April 1944 a party was held for his 46th birthday. A crowd of 8,000 jammed a building in New York to honor Robeson. Thousands more were turned away because the building was full.

Postwar Fight

In 1945 the war ended, and other problems began. The United States and the **Soviet Union** achieved victory after fighting together in World War II. However, they could not agree on what should happen after the war.

The good relationship between the two countries changed. The United States and the Soviet Union had different ideas about how governments should be run. The countries became enemies. They were not at war, but there was a lot of tension between them.

The two countries had very different ways of living. The Soviet Union was a **communist** country, while the United States was a **democracy.** In communist countries the government has control of almost everything, including where people work and live. In contrast, democratic governments allow people a great deal of choice in their everyday lives.

After the war the Soviet Union wanted to introduce other countries to the communist way of life. The Soviets planned to

Paul Robeson sings at a Peace Defense Meeting in the Russian city of Moscow in 1960.

create communist systems in the countries freed by the Americans and the Soviets. But the United States wanted democracy in these countries.

The conflict between the United States and the Soviet Union contributed to a wave of fear among Americans called the "**Red Scare.**" The word "red" is a nickname for a communist. The U.S. government and many Americans were concerned about **communists** at home. Some leaders feared that communists

Robeson was a guest at the 33rd anniversary celebration of the Russian Revolution at the Russian embassy in Washington, D.C., in 1950. No U.S. officials attended the event, but that did not stop Robeson from doing what he believed was right.

wanted to take over the country. Those leaders warned that anybody who supported **communism** could not be trusted.

An Angry Public

In 1947 the U.S. government put Robeson's name on a list of 1,000 people thought to be communists. Robeson refused to change his ideas or his words. He said he was loyal to the United States. He denied that he was a **communist.** However, he said that he was not an enemy of the **Soviet Union,** either. He kept on praising that country for how it treated people equally.

As a result life became very difficult for Robeson. Cities refused to let him perform. Concerts had to be canceled. Robeson finally said he would stop giving concerts for two years. He planned to use all his time to fight for issues he cared about.

Two years later the troubles still had not gone away. In 1949, 85 of his concerts in the United States were canceled. People who planned the shows feared public anger over Robeson's political beliefs. Robeson had to go to England to perform. His concert tour there lasted four months.

Robeson's hardest times were yet to come. Later in 1949, he gave a speech in Paris that made many Americans angry. In the speech he once again praised the way people of color were treated in the Soviet Union. Robeson said that if the United States were to go to war with the Soviets, African Americans would not want to fight against them. American newspapers made it sound as if Robeson did not want African Americans to defend their country.

Later that year, Robeson's son, Pauli, was married in New York. A crowd gathered outside the house where the wedding was held. People booed and hissed when Robeson came out with the wedding party. He was very upset, but a far worse episode was yet to come.

Robeson sings to entertain people gathered in Oregon to support Henry Wallace, a candidate for the 1948 U.S. presidency. Wallace belonged to the progressive party, and Robeson told people that Wallace was the only candidate "interested in our future."

An angry mob decided to stop Robeson from performing later that year. A concert was scheduled for August 27, 1949, in Peekskill, New York. Before it began a mob started a riot at the outdoor concert site. The stage and seats were smashed. A cross was set on fire. People who wanted to hear Robeson sing were attacked. The show had to be canceled. Robeson said he would not be scared away.

Eight days later Robeson gave the concert in Peekskill. He was protected by thousands of members of **labor unions.** Many people still admired Robeson's concern for common people. Workers who were in the unions were still on his side. Still, violence broke out after the concert. More than 100 people were injured.

Robeson and his wife often felt more welcome in the Soviet Union than they did in their home country, the United States. Crowds like this one at a Russian airport on August 17, 1958, were always on hand to welcome them.

Chapter 6:
Later Years

The years after 1950 presented great challenges for Paul Robeson. He had been a great star in earlier times. He had been loved and admired by millions. None of that seemed to matter anymore.

After the violence in Peekskill, Robeson continued on a concert tour of U.S. cities. It was clear that public opinion was divided about him. The courage he showed by performing at Peekskill won support from many African Americans. But he still ran into problems in every city. Many people did not want him to perform. There was no more violence at the shows, but there was tension at every stop.

The U.S. government continued to be suspicious of Robeson. Agents of the Federal Bureau of Investigation kept watch on him. In reality Robeson posed no threat to the United States. He was a loyal American. But his opinions and beliefs were unusual, especially at that time in U.S. history.

Passport Battle

In 1950 the U.S. government took away Robeson's **passport.** The government did so under a new law that took away the rights of people accused of being subversives. A subversive is someone who wants to do away with the ruling government. Robeson denied being a subversive, but it didn't matter. He could not get his passport back, and without it, he could not leave the country.

So Robeson took the government to court. Eventually he was told that he could have his passport back under one condition. He would have to promise not to make any speeches in other countries. Robeson refused to agree. He would not give up his right to free speech.

Robeson had to fight the government in court. It took eight long years for him to win his case. Finally the U.S. Supreme Court ruled in his favor. The government was forced to give him back his passport.

The years in between had been challenging. Robeson was **blacklisted,** which meant that record companies refused to work with him. Concert planners would not let him sing. His income fell from more than $100,000 per year from concerts and records to less than $5,000 per year. He could not get work. The same thing happened to many people who were accused of being **communists.**

Robeson defends himself before the U.S. House of Representatives' Un-American Activities Committee on June 13, 1956. He said the committee members were unpatriotic and told them "You ought to be ashamed of yourselves."

In 1956, Congress called on Robeson to answer questions about his communist activities and beliefs. He refused to answer when someone asked if he was a communist. Someone else asked why Robeson did not go live in the **Soviet Union.** Robeson said he was an American who had the right to speak his mind.

Making a Comeback

Robeson's life turned around in 1958. At the age of 60, he returned to the public eye after a long time away. He published his life story in a book called *Here I Stand*. He also gave a concert in New York, his first in more than ten years. His tour to other cities attracted many African-American fans.

He also enjoyed his freedom to travel. A Supreme Court ruling in June 1958 allowed Robeson and others in his situation to get their **passports** back. He soon left for England, where he gave concerts again. The English welcomed him back and cheered his performances.

He later returned to the **Soviet Union.** Back when Robeson could not leave America, he had become even more famous among the Soviets. They named a mountain in the Soviet Union after Robeson. They also placed a statue of him on the mountaintop. Robeson's 1958 return to the Soviet Union attracted huge crowds of fans.

Robeson's comeback did not stop there. In 1959 he went back to England to perform in a play. It was *Othello* again. He played the part that had made him famous years earlier. In 1960 he went on a concert tour with his old friend Lawrence Brown. They performed in Australia and New Zealand. It was the last time they would tour together.

Robeson speaks in Moscow in 1949 to help celebrate the 150th anniversary of the birth of a famous Russian poet, Alexander Pushkin. Talks like these in Russian cities are one of the reasons why many Americans thought Robeson was a communist.

The Final Years

Unfortunately Robeson had health problems during his comeback. He spent time in a hospital in 1959 because of exhaustion. He barely recovered in time to perform in *Othello*. His wife also had been ill.

In 1963 Robeson and his wife both checked into a clinic in Berlin, Germany. Doctors diagnosed Robeson with a bone disorder.

Essie found out she had cancer. The couple returned to the United States. Robeson's days of travel and fame were over.

He spent much of his time with Essie in Harlem. She fought cancer for two more years. She died on December 13, 1965, two days before her 70th birthday.

Robeson's health was very poor at that time. After Essie's death he moved to Philadelphia, to the home of his sister, Marian Robeson Forsythe. Marian, four years his elder, took care of Robeson for the rest of his life. He never appeared in public again.

A celebration was planned for his 75th birthday in 1973. The event was held at Carnegie Hall in New York City. Robeson was too sick to attend, but tickets sold out just the same. The crowd listened to recordings of Robeson singing and watched him on film. On stage many famous African Americans spoke in his honor. Sydney Poitier and James Earl Jones were among them. Both are great African-American actors who followed in Robeson's footsteps.

Robeson sent a tape of a special message to the audience. On the tape, he said, "I want you to remember that I am the same old Paul, dedicated as ever to . . . freedom, peace, and brotherhood."

After suffering a stroke, Robeson died on January 23, 1976, in a Philadelphia hospital. He was 77.

Sidney Poitier

Paul Robeson's success helped pave the way for many other African-American performers. He showed that African Americans could be stars and win fans of all colors.

Sidney Poitier was one of the actors who followed in Robeson's footsteps. Poitier became one of the most important African-American actors in history.

Sidney Poitier poses in 1964 with the Oscar he won for Best Performance by an Actor for his role in the movie Lilies *of the Field.*

Born in 1925, Poitier got his first acting job in the late 1940s. In 1958 he became the first African American to be nominated for an Academy Award for Best Actor for his role in *The Defiant One*s. He did not win the award that year, but his luck was different five years later. In 1963 he won the Academy Award for Best Actor for his part in a movie called *Lilies of the Field.* Since then he has starred in dozens of movies and plays. He blazed a trail for others, just as Robeson had done for him.

This photo of Robeson in the play Showboat *was sent with other photos to him and his wife. His wife wrote to the photographer to say she thought the picture was excellent. She wrote, "The others are not so good . . . because his smile is a little too set."*

Chapter 7: Robeson's Place in History

Paul Robeson's story began with his family. He was closest to his father, who was a former slave. His father made Robeson believe that anything was possible. His father helped him study and prepare for life on his own.

Robeson was a gifted person in many ways. He made use of every one of his skills. He was a great student, athlete, actor, singer, and leader. He also used his gifts to aid others who were less fortunate.

His place in history is still changing. During his lifetime he became one of the most famous people in the world. He also endured difficult years and watched his fame fade away. Many people treated him with anger and scorn. For years he was all but forgotten by the American public.

Before his death, though, Robeson won back many fans. It has been more than 25 years since he died. Since then many more people have learned about Robeson and his accomplishments. Thousands of people now admire his talents as a singer and actor.

But even today some people believe that Robeson's contributions have not been fully recognized. They think that Robeson would be much more famous if it had not been for his political beliefs and the government's treatment of him during the **Red Scare.** Others claim that his fame has lasted, but only among African Americans. They think whites and others still need to learn about Robeson and give him credit for all he did.

But one thing is certain: Robeson accomplished great things that cannot be forgotten. He was one of the top college athletes of his generation. He was a brilliant performer on stage. His work opened the doors for many African-Americans in the arts. He was a firm believer in the equality of all people. His efforts in the 1930s and 1940s helped make it possible for later generations of African Americans to win equal rights.

By the time he visited Budapest, Hungary, in 1959, Robeson had many admirers and fans, like these children, who knew of his struggles and his talents and came out to give him their support.

Glossary

blacklisted to be identified publicly as someone who should not be given work due to his or her political views

communism political system in which all goods and property are owned by the government and divided among the people

communist person who believes in communism

democracy system of government in which the people choose their leaders in elections

discrimination unfair treatment of people because of how they look or who they are

Great Depression period beginning in 1929 and lasting through the 1930s during which many U.S. businesses failed and many people were out of work

labor union group of workers who join together to bargain for better pay and better treatment on the job

Nazi Party political group in Germany led by Adolf Hitler, whose actions were among the major causes of World War II

Nazi   member of the Nazi Party

passport   official booklet that proves you are a citizen of a certain country and allows you to travel abroad

plantation   large farm in the South. Until the end of the Civil War, the work on plantations was usually done by slaves

prejudice   negative attitude toward others, often based on race

Red Scare   period in the 1950s when communists living in the United States were thought to be a serious threat

scholarship   grant or prize that pays for college or some other course of study

segregation   act of keeping groups of different people, such as races or religions, separate

Soviet Union   former country in Europe and Asia. It included Russia and several other current countries.

spiritual   traditional African-American song

stereotype   fixed idea about how a person or group behaves

Timeline

1898 - Paul Leroy Robeson is born on April 9 to Reverend William and Maria Robeson in Princeton, New Jersey. He is the youngest of five children.

1915- Wins a scholarship to Rutgers University. He is the third African American to attend the college.

1922 - Gets his first professional acting job in a play called *Taboo.*

1925 - Robeson and friend Lawrence Brown give a concert of old African-American **spirituals.**

1935 - Visits the Soviet Union and is impressed by how fairly people of color seem to be treated.

1943 - Completes a successful concert tour in the United States and stars in *Othello* on Broadway in New York City.

1947 - Announces he will stop giving concerts for two years and spend his time fighting for an end to racial **prejudice.**

1949 - Gives a speech about the Soviet Union in Paris that angers some in the United States. Many of his concerts are canceled back home, and a riot breaks out at his show in Peekskill, New York.

1950 - U.S. government lists Robeson as a **communist** and takes away his passport. Robeson takes the government to court.

1958 - U.S. Supreme Court rules in Robeson's favor. His passport is returned. His autobiography, *Here I Stand,* is published.

1963 - Robeson and his wife return to United States after five years abroad.

1964 - Robeson's wife dies of cancer.

1976 - Robeson dies on January 23 at age 77.

Further Information

Further reading

McKissak, Patricia C., et al. *Paul Robeson: A Voice to Remember.* Berkeley Heights, N.J.: Enslow Publishers, 2001.

Samuels, Steve, et al. *Paul Robeson: Singer and Actor.* Broomall, Penn.: Chelsea House, 1989.

Stewart, Jeffrey C., et al. *Paul Robeson: Artist and Citizen.* New Brunswick, N.J.: Rutgers, 1998.

Addresses

Rutgers University
Room 202
65 Davidson Road
Piscataway, NJ 08854-809

Paul Robeson Cultural Center
600 Bartholomew Road
Piscataway, NJ 08854

National Association for the Advancement of Colored People (NAACP)
4805 Mount Hope Drive
Baltimore, MD 21215

Index